Mary Barmeyer O'Brien

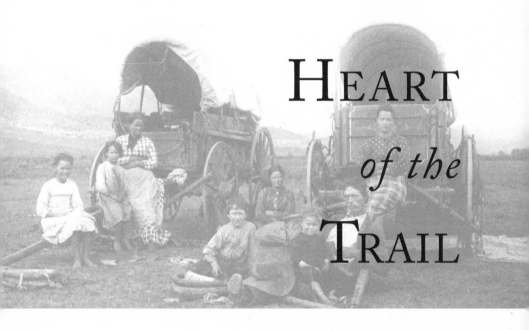

HEART
of the
TRAIL

The Stories of Eight Wagon Train Women

TWODOT

HELENA, MONTANA

A · TWODOT · BOOK

© 1997 Mary Barmeyer O'Brien

Published by Falcon® Publishing, Inc.
Helena, Montana

Cover photo courtesy of Denver Public Library/Western History Department.

10 9 8 7 6

Printed in the United States of America.

Design, typesetting, and other prepress work by Falcon, Helena, Montana.

Library of Congress Cataloging-in-Publication Data

O'Brien, Mary Barmeyer.
    Heart of the trail : the stories of eight wagon train women / Mary
Barmeyer O'Brien.
       p.   cm.
    "A TwoDot book"—T.p. verso.
    Includes bibliographical references and index.
    ISBN 1-56044-562-9
    1. Women pioneers—West (U.S.)—Biography. 2. Overland journeys
to the Pacific. 3. Frontier and pioneer life—West (U.S.) 4. West
(U.S.)—Biography. 5. West (U.S.)—Description and travel.
I. Title.
F593.O27 1997
978'.02'09022—dc21
[B]   97-25402
                                       CIP

Falcon® Publishing, Inc.
P. O. Box 1718, Helena, MT 59624

For my family, one and all.

CONTENTS

ACKNOWLEDGMENTS

Heartfelt thanks to those who have contributed to the successful completion of this book, especially:

—the staff at Polson City Library, Marilyn Trosper, Connie Cummings, and Linda Allen, for their diligent, unfailing assistance which has been gratefully appreciated;

—friend and fellow writer Maggie Plummer, for her expert help and faithful encouragement;

—Megan Hiller, my editor at Falcon, for her support and fine work;

—my family and friends, for their constant interest and good wishes;

—the many archivists, curators, and librarians along the way, for their expertise and assistance, including: Eleanor M. Gehres, Manager of the Western History/Genealogy Department of the Denver Public Library; Karyl Winn, Curator of Manuscripts, University of Washington Libraries, Seattle; Richard T. Read, University Archivist/Museum Curator at Pacific University, Forest Grove, Oregon; the staff and volunteers at California's Huntington and Bancroft Libraries; Connie Geiger, Archival Technician at the Montana Historical Society; the staff and volunteers at the End of the Oregon Trail Interpretive Center in Oregon City, Oregon; at the Replica of Old Fort Hall in Pocatello, Idaho; and at the Clark County Historical Museum in Vancouver, Washington;

—and the eight pioneer women who inspired this book by sharing their stories with us.

Special Note: I would especially like to thank the following archival sources for their kind assistance in providing materials:

University of Washington Libraries for information on Amelia Stewart Knight.

The Denver Public Library for information on Julia Anna Archibald (Holmes).

Pacific University Archives for information on Tabitha Moffat Brown.

Many of the women in this book have published letters and diaries which are cited in the bibliographies at the end of each chapter. Occasionally, I have used the women's own words to help tell their stories. All excerpts from the letters and diaries are presented as closely to the original as possible, including unusual spellings, punctuation, and grammar.

INTRODUCTION

When covered wagons began crawling west from the Missouri River in the 1840s, their white canvas tops billowed against the huge sky and their iron-rimmed wheels carried emigrants into a land that was unspoiled and spectacular. First came the wide green prairies, where delicate wildflowers and native grasses, some as high as a horse's head, grew undisturbed. Teeming with prairie dogs, jack rabbits, deer, and bison, the prairies stretched for hundreds of miles to the west. Finally, mountains jutted up from the plains, and tangled forests filled the air with the fragrance of pine. Bald eagles swooped over clear, pristine lakes to feed on fish. Elsewhere, deserts in delicate natural balance shimmered in the baking sun. Thousands of Native Americans inhabited this enormous land. Throughout the centuries, they had become adept at surviving on the West's dramatic terrain.

To the east of the wide, muddy Mississippi River, people were searching for better opportunities. In the late 1830s, a prolonged depression settled over the United States. Wages fell and there was widespread unemployment. It wasn't long before people began to feel crowded, too, and disease became more common. By the 1860s, the problems of the Civil War were weighing heavily upon northerners and southerners alike.

During those years, the West seemed like a land of promise. Potential emigrants had been told that free land, gold, and a new beginning awaited them. By the thousands, people of all backgrounds sold their homes and farms, loaded their often unwilling families into covered wagons, and started out.

Immediately they found the stunning western landscape could be as harsh as it was spectacular. Hundreds of miles of rugged routes stretched to the horizon crossing rushing rivers and treacherous mountain passes, as well as long barren stretches without life-giving water or food. The pioneers worked themselves to the bone carving trails through the almost impassible wilderness. But to reach the West, it seemed worth the intense struggle.

Native Americans, though, saw the mass emigration in a different light as their homelands were invaded and ultimately settled by these travelers who thought the frontier was free for the taking.

For about thirty years—from the early 1840s to the late 1860s—the Oregon Trail, the Santa Fe Trail, the Bozeman Trail, and dozens of other perilous routes were the sites of possibly the hardest, most immense migration of all time. Wagon train after wagon train inched over the poor roads. Most pioneers endured overwhelming hardships to complete their long journeys—journeys they hoped would improve their lives and the lives of their children.

Women played an extraordinary role in the westward movement, but sometimes their contributions and sacrifices were overlooked. As their covered wagons jolted them over the two-thousand-mile-long trails, they had to summon every bit of their strength and courage just to survive. They knew they had left friends and family behind, in many cases forever. For most women, it was not their decision to travel off into an unknown land far from the schools and churches they cherished. But of necessity they toiled on, bearing children and raising families on the unrelenting trail.

Perhaps such women recognized what an astonishing undertaking their journeys were, because many stole a few minutes each day from their never-ending work to write diaries or letters about their trip.

Others wrote memoirs long after their journeys were over. Many times their writings contrasted with the diaries and letters of their fathers, husbands, and brothers. Pioneer men often wrote about such concerns as finding camping places with good grass and water for their livestock, covering as many miles as possible, hunting, or fixing broken wagons. Women, on the other hand, generally focused on the human side of the trip: the children, families, and fellow travelers. They frequently wrote about trying to keep their loved ones safe and healthy, helping where there was sickness and death, and making new friendships. They recorded the joys of new births, weddings, and campfire dances. While the men mostly oversaw the necessities of wagons, animals, and routes, it was the women who were the heart of the trail.

Today, along with the deep ruts their wagon wheels carved into the earth, many of their remarkable written records still exist. Among them are the works of most of the resourceful women selected for the following pages. Along with the larger lessons they share with us, these women answer our questions about covered wagon life. How did they roll out pie crust in the wilderness or churn butter in an overcrowded wagon? We learn how they avoided mosquito bites, washed clothes on river banks, and cared faithfully for their children. We share their overwhelming grief as death claimed those dear to them, their joy at the unequaled scenery, and their misery as they huddled in cold wet beds under leaking canvas wagon covers.

From Amelia Knight, who gave birth to her eighth child on the Oregon Trail, to Sarah Royce, who faced death from thirst in the merciless desert, to Grandma Brown, who had to abandon her wagon and continue her exhausting trip on horseback, these exceptional women arouse our admiration for their sheer grit and endurance. Without a doubt, they earned their niche in history with their sacrifices, failures, and contributions. We remember them for the legacies they left.

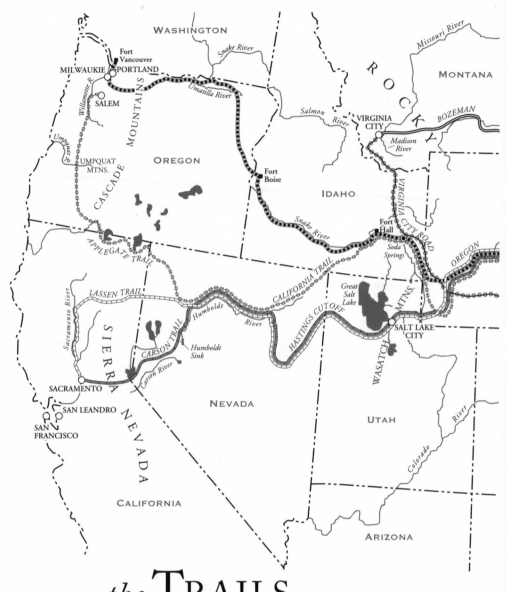

the TRAILS

```
0            150           300
```

Scale of Miles

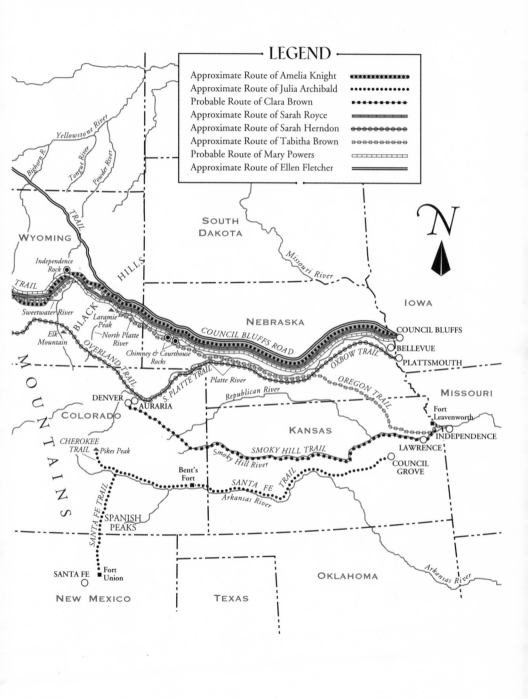

N

WYOMING

SOUTH DAKOTA

Yellowstone River

Bighorn R.

Tongue River

Powder River

TRAIL

Independence Rock

BLACK HILLS

Missouri River

Sweetwater River

TRAIL

Laramie Peak

North Platte River

Elk Mountain

OVERLAND TRAIL

Chimney & Courthouse Rocks

COUNCIL BLUFFS ROAD

NEBRASKA

IOWA

COUNCIL BLUFFS

BELLEVUE

PLATTSMOUTH

OXBOW TRAIL

S. PLATTE TRAIL

Platte River

Republican River

OREGON TRAIL

MISSOURI

DENVER

AURARIA

COLORADO

Fort Leavenworth

KANSAS

INDEPENDENCE

MOUNTAINS

CHEROKEE TRAIL

Pikes Peak

Smoky Hill River

SMOKY HILL TRAIL

LAWRENCE

COUNCIL GROVE

Bent's Fort

SANTA FE TRAIL

Arkansas River

SANTA FE TRAIL

SPANISH PEAKS

SANTA FE

Fort Union

NEW MEXICO

OKLAHOMA

Arkansas River

TEXAS

OUTLASTING THE OREGON TRAIL
The Story of Amelia Stewart Knight

"Lucy!" Amelia Knight called. Her voice was frantic as she searched up and down the dusty wagon train for her eight-year-old daughter. "Lucy Jane!"

Of all the hardships Amelia and her large family had encountered along the Oregon Trail, none compared to losing Lucy. Where could her little girl be? Amelia scanned the hot, dry countryside scattered only with sparse sagebrush and boulders.

It was August 8, 1853. When the travelers broke camp and turned their heavy wagons onto the trail that morning, Amelia thought Lucy was riding in her usual place inside the family's second wagon. But Lucy wasn't there, and no one had noticed she hadn't climbed aboard. The hired driver had seen she wasn't in her usual spot. But when he'd asked, he was told the child was in the first wagon with her mother. Now that they had stopped to rest the tired oxen, they realized they had left Lucy behind. She was all alone in this vast, wild country, somewhere back down the trail.

It had been a long, difficult trip for Amelia Stewart Knight, her husband Joel (who was a doctor), and their seven children: Plutarch (age seventeen), Seneca (fifteen), Frances (fourteen), Jefferson (eleven), Lucy (eight), Almira (five), and Chatfield (two). They knew the two-thousand-mile overland trip from their home in Iowa to western Washington was not a journey for the weak or timid. Problem after problem plagued those who struggled over the dangerous route. There was thick dust to choke them, rain to soak their bodies and belongings, and wild windstorms which sometimes tipped over their wagons and scattered their few precious supplies across the prairie. Long, remote sections of trail without firewood or supplies stretched on and on. Moreover, the weary travelers had to endure biting insects, day after day of the same tedious food, rattlesnakes, and the threat of deadly illness with limited medical care and supplies. For Amelia Knight, most of the difficulties could be patiently endured. But leaving Lucy behind was another matter. She could picture her small daughter, terrified and alone beside the untamed river where they had camped last night.

Suddenly Amelia's breath caught with hope. Lumbering up the trail behind them was another wagon train. Perhaps the newcomers had discovered Lucy and brought her along. As the wagons got closer, Amelia could see that little Lucy was indeed with them! With joy, the family ran to greet her and thank the travelers who had reunited their family.

When the Knights left Iowa on April 9, 1853, they were well prepared for the grueling trip ahead. They were healthy and fully stocked with provisions and plenty of fresh oxen, including their faithful team, Tip and Tyler. Reports say the family had three wagons and five hired men to accompany them. Within just a week, though, two of the children had mumps, and Amelia had such a terrible headache that she was sick, too. Pouring rain had drenched their belongings and turned the wagon road into deep mud. Then three of the horses escaped and had to be tracked down in the cold wind.

Amelia probably knew that all this was just the beginning of the

AMELIA STEWART KNIGHT
OREGON HISTORICAL SOCIETY, #59564

hardships. Maybe that is why she recorded nearly every day's events in her diary. In her clear firm handwriting, she put down the facts—but hardly ever her feelings—about the cross-country journey. She didn't complain, but simply related the daily happenings in a matter-of-fact way. Her plain, truthful descriptions show vividly what it was like to travel the Oregon Trail.

(April 23, 1853) Still in camp, it rained hard all night, and blew a hurrican almost, all the tents were blown down, and some wagons capsized, Evening it has been raining hard all day, every thing is wet and muddy, One of the oxen missing, the boys have been hunting him all day. Dreary times, wet and muddy, and crowded in the tent, cold and wet and uncomfortable in the wagon no place for the poor children . . .

It was indeed a rainy spring, and as the wagons traveled, the heavy wheels bogged down in soft mudholes. Camping was miserable. Soon after crossing the Missouri River at Council Bluffs and starting across the flat Nebraska plains, Amelia described an especially wretched windy night when everyone went to sleep ". . . in wet beds, with their wet clothes on, without supper . . ."

During the entire journey, which took more than five months, Amelia's hours were packed with endless chores. She had no choice but to put in a full day's work beginning before sunrise, even when she was sick. On May 24 she wrote: ". . . weather pleasant, I had the sick headache all night, some better this morning, must do a days work . . ." Her chores included mending and scrubbing the few plain clothes the family had brought along and keeping an ever watchful eye on her youngest children, especially two-year-old Chatfield. Preparing meals for her family of nine and their five hired hands took much of Amelia's time. She rarely wrote about being tired, though she must have been as she labored her way across the continent. During the entire trip she was expecting another baby—her eighth child—a fact never mentioned in her diary.

Like many busy frontier women, Amelia took time to appreciate the beauty of the land around her. As the party left Nebraska and entered what is now Wyoming, she jotted in her diary: "There is some splendid scenery here, beautiful vallies, and dark green clad hills, with their ledges of rock, and then far away over them you can see Larimie peak, with her snow capt top . . ."

The weather did its best to discourage the Knights. As the cold, wet, muddy spring ended, the days got warmer. Soon the family baked in disagreeable heat. Dust storms whirled with force across the bone-dry land. Amelia told of getting breakfast one day in the driving wind and grit, writing in her diary that whoever ate the most breakfast ate the most sand. The wagons in front of the Knights also stirred up thick clouds of dust. During the dry summer weeks, the wagons, belongings, and travelers were covered with powdery dirt. Earlier wagon trains had trampled and overgrazed the long grasses and formed ruts. But even though the wagons fanned out to avoid following each other, the choking grit was everywhere. One evening in June, Amelia wrote in exasperation ". . . I have just washed the dust out of my eyes so that I can see to get supper . . ."

Mile by difficult mile, the wagon train toiled westward.

(June 11, 1853) . . . not a drop of water, not a spear of grass to be seen, nothing but barren hills, bare broken rocks, sand and dust. . . . We reached platte river about noon, and our cattle were so crazy for water, that some of them plunged headlong into the river with their yokes on . . .

By mid-June they had gone only as far as Independence Rock

and the Sweetwater River in the center of present-day Wyoming. Covering just a few miles a day, they climbed over mountain passes where snowbanks were six feet deep, crept across the countryside, and hauled the wagons through steep, hot ravines.

On the Fourth of July (a travel day like any other), Amelia's thermometer read 110 degrees. On top of that, little Chat had a fever, which his mother thought was partly caused by the swarms of mosquitos biting him. Usually Amelia would have covered him with veils and extra clothing to keep the irritating insects off, but the blistering sun was too hot. All they could do was push on, slowly making their way into southern Idaho.

Even in dry country, the wagons had to ford occasional streams and broad, deep rivers. At the confluence of the Salmon and Snake rivers on today's Idaho/Oregon border, Amelia wrote: " . . . a frightful place, with the water roarring and tumbling ten or 15 feet below it. . . . here we have to unload all the wagons and pack every thing across by hand, and then we are only on an Island there is a worse place to cross yet . . ."

Although there were long arid stretches between streams, only a little water could be carried in the wagons because it added so much weight. Over and over, Amelia's diary mentions the all-important search for daily water. Sometimes, when the tired travelers did find a spring or creek, it was not safe to drink from because of alkali (mineral salt) deposits. Fresh grass and feed for the livestock were just as critical. Amelia wrote that she and Joel fed flour and meal to their horses and cattle when they ran out of feed. Dead stock littered the Oregon Trail and the animals that plodded on had sore feet or necks that bled from rubbing on their yokes.

But as the Knights crept over the long wagon road, Amelia remembered to write about the simple pleasures that brought the family joy and comfort. She mentioned that her husband once gathered her a bright bouquet of wildflowers. Another time, they happily discovered tangy, fresh wild currants. Amelia made "a nice lot of currant pies" that afternoon. They also savored the fresh fish and potatoes they sometimes bought from the Native Americans they encountered along the way.

By late August, the party had tackled eastern Oregon and the Blue Mountains, but it would take another long month to reach their destination. Just ahead lay the barren, parched Umatilla Valley. The livestock were by then so tired and weak that pulling the heavy wagons in the scorching sun would kill them, so the group traveled at night and in the cool early mornings. Wood was scarce, but Amelia was able to make her cooking fires with wild sagebrush.

The Knights encountered the most rugged part of the trail in the densely vegetated Cascade Mountains.

(September 8, 1853) Traveled 14 miles over the worst road that was ever made up and down very steep rough and rocky hills, through mud holes, twisting and winding round stumps, logs, and fallen trees. now we are on the end of a log, now bounce down in a mud hole, now over a big root of a tree, or rock, then bang goes the other side of the wagon and woe to be whatever is inside . . .

(September 9, 1853) There is no end to the wagons, buggys ox yokes, chains, ect that are lying all along this road some splendid good wagons just left standing . . .

Other travelers had to abandon their covered wagons, but the Knight family was able to get theirs through to the end of the trip. Amelia did tell of leaving her pickles and a few other belongings behind on the trail, since they were too "unhandy" to carry. At one point, they split up the wagon's deck boards to make firewood and to lighten the load. Here again, Amelia threw out "a good many things."

By mid-September, the family could see the journey's end. Near Milwaukie, Oregon, just across the Columbia River from their destination, the drizzling rain began again, and Amelia wrote with what seems to have been great weariness: (September 13) "We may now call ourselves through, they say. Here we are in Oregon making our camp in an ugly bottom, with no home, except our wagons and tent, it is drizzling and the weather looks dark and gloomy . . ." After four more rainy days, Amelia's diary ends. Her eighth child was born the next day. She named him Wilson Carl Knight after the hired driver of their second wagon.

Soon after Amelia gave birth, the tired family ferried across the Columbia River to the new Territory of Washington, a process that is said to have taken three days. There, about ten miles upstream from Vancouver, Washington, they are believed to have traded two yokes of oxen for a piece of land partially planted in potatoes and a small log cabin. This is where they made their new home, which would become the family farm for many years.

Amelia was well educated for the time, and she taught and encouraged her children to study. They grew up to become prominent citizens. Her husband Joel was reportedly active in community affairs. He often represented Clark County at the Territorial Legislature. In 1867, fourteen years after the family settled in Washington, Joel died of tuberculosis. Amelia remarried, but her second marriage did not last. She was elderly when she died in 1896 and was buried beside Joel in the Knight Cemetery on the north bank of the Columbia River.

Today we can picture Amelia on the westward journey, exhausted but resolute, sitting beside her battered wagon, writing in her diary by smoky firelight. With her youngest children asleep, she could take a few minutes to sink onto the prairie with her pen in her callused hand, to write down the day's events. Other times, she probably wrote while cramped in the damp, dark family tent, or sitting in the stifling heat of the sunbaked wagon. Her well-chosen words probably seemed ordinary to her then. Little did she know that generations later we would read them and be inspired by her patience, by her sheer hard work, and by the way she and her family outlasted the Oregon Trail. ▨

Specific Sources for Amelia Stewart Knight's Story

Clark County Pioneers: A Centennial Salute. Vancouver, Washington: Clark County Genealogical Society, 1989, p. 406–409.

Eide, Ingvard Henry, editor and photographer. *Oregon Trail.* Chicago, New York, San Francisco: Rand McNally & Company, 1972.

Knight, Amelia. Pioneer diary as published in *Covered Wagon Women/ Diaries and Letters from the Western Trail 1840 - 1890*, volume VI, edited and compiled by Kenneth L. Holmes. Glendale, California: The Arthur H. Clark Company, 1986.

To the Summit in Bloomers

The Story of Julia Anna Archibald (Holmes)

The shaggy new bison calf was hungry. Twenty-year-old Julia felt sorry for the frightened creature, especially when she heard that the wagon train's hunters had shot and killed its mother. Now, tied near the covered wagons, it gave a soft cry. Without hesitation, Julia mixed up some flour and water—the only things she had for a small bison to drink—and slowly approached the animal. But as she got close, the little calf lowered its head and butted her so hard she lost her balance. The flour and water mixture slopped onto the prairie grass.

No one knows whether Julia tried to feed him again, nor what became of him, because she did not mention him again in the letters she wrote during her covered wagon trip in 1858. In the beautifully written accounts she sent to her mother and to a small feminist newspaper in the East, Julia Anna Archibald described the journey she took from Lawrence, Kansas to the gold fields at Pike's Peak.**

---

* In keeping with her belief in equal rights, Julia often used her maiden name instead of the surname of her husband, Holmes.

**Although the accepted spelling today is "Pikes Peak," the early usage included an apostrophe: "Pike's Peak."

Her poetic writings tell of her summer's ox-cart trip on the Santa Fe Trail.

She traveled with her new husband, who was a bold and daring man named James Henry Holmes, and her eighteen-year-old brother, Albert W. Archibald. Young, hopeful, and adventurous in spirit, the three hoped to find gold at the end of their trip, but were even more anxious to see the spectacular Rocky Mountains.

Julia was a pretty, intelligent woman who believed that men and women should be treated equally. Julia's attitudes and writings were influenced by her mother, who was a women's rights supporter and a personal friend of the famous pioneer of the women's movement, Susan B. Anthony, and by her father, an anti-slavery activist. Julia, or "Annie" as she was sometimes called, was proud of her bold decision not to wear the traditional long dresses on the trail, but to wear bloomers (a short skirt over a pair of baggy pants) instead. Even though bloomers were considered somewhat scandalous, Julia felt the full, toe-length dresses of the day would get in her way on the long journey. She enjoyed wandering through the deep, waving grasses in search of colorful wildflowers, and felt her comfortable bloomers gave her the freedom to do that.

As the wagons set out on their journey, she wrote:

Nearly all the men were entire strangers to me, and as I was cooking our dinner some of them crowded around our wagon, gazing sometimes at the stove . . . but oftener on my dress, which did not surprise me, for, I presume, some of them had never seen just such a costume before.

Julia felt so strongly about wearing bloomers that she had trouble forming a friendship with the only other woman on the wagon train, Mrs. Middleton, who wore long skirts. When they discussed their difference, Mrs. Middleton begged Julia to wear traditional clothing because the men of the party talked among themselves about how odd bloomers looked. Julia replied that she could not dress to please others.

Julia also asked the wagon train's guardmaster if she could take her turn at guarding the camp, traditionally a job for men only:

> . . . I signified to the Guardmaster that I desired to take my turn with the others in the duty of guarding the camp, and requested to have my watch assigned with my husband. The captain of the guard . . . was of the opinion that it would be a disgrace to the gentlemen of the company for them to permit a woman to stand on guard.

Julia, although disturbed at the guardmaster's refusal, turned her attention to other things. She began studying wildflowers, writing in her journal, teaching her brother the Lord's Prayer in Spanish, and consciously improving her physical fitness by walking longer and longer distances each day.

Meanwhile the wagons pressed on. Julia wrote about the presence of Native Americans—Cheyenne and Arapaho—describing them in her letters as "large, finely formed, and noble looking men" who visited the wagon train bringing messages or wanting to trade with the travelers.

For about three hundred miles, the wagons roughly followed the Arkansas River. Julia commented that although the river was scenic, "the current is so swift that it is very unpleasant bathing—that delightful and grateful recreation to the dusty traveler." By late June, the travelers had reached Bent's Fort, a large adobe fortress with four-foot-thick walls, located on a bluff overlooking the upper Arkansas River in what is now Colorado. A few days later, on the Fourth of

JULIA ANNA ARCHIBALD (HOLMES)
DENVER PUBLIC LIBRARY, WESTERN HISTORY DEPARTMENT

July and just a month after the wagons started out, a snowy mountain appeared in the distance. Reaching high into the sky, it stood out from the rest of the majestic Rockies. Pike's Peak! It was their destination, and they felt sure they would find treasured gold among its foothills.

Four days later, they camped as close to the mountains as they could get in the heavy wagons. They would remain there for more than a month while the prospectors among them, who were mostly inexperienced, made excursions to look for gold, and others attempted to hunt game. Oddly enough, Julia's letters didn't mention whether or not she and James and her brother spent time searching for gold, nor if they found any.

Although to her knowledge no woman and very few men had ever made the hazardous and difficult climb to the snowy summit of Pike's Peak, she and her husband decided to do so. Julia was in strong physical condition from her miles of long walks. Late in July, tiring of the monotony of camp life, Julia filled her backpack with hiking supplies including food, a quilt, and some clothing. James carried food, camping gear, some writing materials, and a treasured book of Ralph Waldo Emerson's essays. They planned to be gone for six days.

In her journal, Julia recorded the highlights of the climb, beginning on August 1, 1858. At first they hiked through the undisturbed foothills, crossing at least one knee-deep stream so cold it made her feet ache. Then they reached the mountain itself. Julia thrilled at the fragrant evergreens, the crystal clear mountain creeks tumbling and foaming down the ravines, and the variety of "bewitchingly beautiful" wildflowers.

By August 4, Julia and James had climbed to within two steep miles of the summit. They made a base camp on the mountainside where they could see distant covered wagons and tents on the great hazy plains below. There, in a mossy sheltered place they named

15

Snowdell, they spent a day writing, resting, and admiring the landscape. The next day, August 5, they set off for the rocky peak, carrying only their writing materials and their Emerson book. Near the top, the climb became much harder as they came upon huge, steep piles of stones, difficult to scale.

When the couple finally reached the cold windy summit of Pike's Peak at an altitude of more than 14,000 feet, Julia rejoiced in their accomplishment. She felt she was possibly the first woman ever to stand at the top. Shivering but exultant, they left their names on a large boulder and stayed to write some letters. Julia put down these words to her mother:

I have accomplished the task which I marked out for myself, and now I feel amply repaid for all my toil and fatigue. Nearly every one tried to discourage me from attempting it, but I believed that I should succeed; and now here I am, and feel that I would not have missed this glorious sight for anything at all.

Before leaving the summit, Julia read aloud some beloved words from Emerson, and then they hurried partway down the vast mountain in a summer snowstorm. The next day, tired but fulfilled, they arrived back at the wagon train.

The prospectors in the party, despite their inexperience, apparently did discover a small amount of gold at Pike's Peak, which perhaps drew others to the area. Later on, several larger gold strikes were made nearby. But most of the group, including Julia and her husband and brother, wanted to push on to New Mexico in search of bigger deposits. Nearly all of them turned their wagons toward the warm Spanish Peaks area to continue hunting gold during the winter.

Julia and James spent the next few years in New Mexico, where James was appointed Secretary of the Territory by President Lincoln, and Julia was a correspondent for the *New York Herald Tribune*. They eventually had four children: two sons and two daughters. During the last years of the Civil War the family moved to Washington, D.C., where Julia and James were divorced. There Julia lived out her life working in federal agencies and continuing her efforts on behalf of women's organizations.

Today we remember Julia standing strong and determined at the lofty summit of Pike's Peak, with her bloomer costume flapping in the icy wind. Looking east, she could see the brown plains she had crossed to reach her destination. But looking west, she saw new frontiers: frontiers that offered hope for the ideals of feminism she held dear. With her independent thinking and the words she wrote on her pioneer journey, Julia Anna Archibald helped bring the issue of women's rights to the American West. 🌸

Specific Sources for Julia Anna Archibald (Holmes)'s Story

Archibald (Holmes), Julia Anna. Pioneer letters as published in *Covered Wagon Women/ Diaries and Letters from the Western Trail 1840 -1890*, volume VII, edited and compiled by Kenneth L. Holmes. Glendale, California: The Arthur H. Clark Company, 1988.

Grant, Bruce. *Famous American Trails*. Chicago, New York, San Francisco: Rand McNally & Company, 1973.

Lavender, David. *Bent's Fort*. Garden City, New York: Doubleday & Co., Inc., 1954.

Spring, Agnes Wright. *A Bloomer Girl on Pike's Peak* 1858. Denver: Western History Department, Denver Public Library, 1949.

I Lift My Lamp*

The Story of Clara Brown

Clara Brown skillfully turned the savory bison roast in the heavy Dutch oven and heaped on more campfire coals. She needed to stew some dried apples and bake more biscuits, too—enough to provide dinner and breakfast for a large group of hungry men. The wagon drivers for whom she was hired to cook could gobble up a whole buttery biscuit in a single mouthful! Even though she'd be working late tonight, she would be up again tomorrow long before dawn.

All day, Clara had trudged beside the covered wagons. The ground under her aching feet was dusty that hot day in 1859, and the sun beat down on her dark skin. But she held her graying head high and her back straight, as she walked, one step after another, to her new home in the West.

Clara was a recently freed African-American slave in her late fifties. Historical accounts differ about whether Clara was set free by a family who loved and respected her or whether she finally saved enough money to buy her own freedom, but afterwards she moved to

---

* "I lift my lamp beside the golden door."—from the inscription for the Statue of Liberty by Emma Lazarus.

Leavenworth, Kansas Territory. There she worked as a household cook and a laundress.

Years before her emancipation, Clara had endured the most terrible of heartbreaks: her husband, her son, and her two living daughters had been sold away from her. Clara was left with a permanent empty place in her heart. Only her steadfast faith in God sustained her. From what she could learn now, it seemed that just one of her beloved family was still alive: her grown daughter Eliza Jane. Clara's fondest dream was to find her someday.

Clara wondered if Eliza Jane might be in Colorado where people were flocking by the thousands seeking gold. When she heard about a freight company of covered wagons hauling goods from Leavenworth to Pike's Peak, she asked to go along as far as Denver. The freighters agreed, if she would cook for some of the company's men on the eight-week journey. Researchers believe that she, like the others, walked the entire seven hundred miles since the wagons would have been packed to the brim with freight and supplies.

Details about Clara Brown's trip west are scarce. Since she was born into slavery, she had little opportunity to learn to read or write. No diary or letters about her journey have ever been found. But we can safely assume that she cooked wild game and biscuits on the trail, as nearly all pioneer women did, and that she used common staples: salt pork and bacon to supplement the fresh game, hundreds of pounds of flour and sugar, rice, beans, baking soda, salt, and coffee. Most wagons carried water kegs as well. Clara's cooking gear might have included at least one large kettle, skillets, and a big coffee pot along with tin dishes and cups.

Although meals on the westward journey were usually plain and monotonous, women like Clara tried to add variety. Sometimes they formed cooked beans into a loaf which could be used as sandwich filler. If they found wild duck or goose eggs, they made simple cakes

CLARA BROWN
DENVER PUBLIC LIBRARY, WESTERN HISTORY DEPARTMENT

or custards. Some brought a few luxuries from home: canned oysters, pickles, or molasses. Others included dried fruit, vinegar, or wild berries to prevent scurvy. Being an experienced cook, Clara probably knew many tricks to create flavorful trail food. But her successes wouldn't have come without hardship. Pioneer women reported that their pots, which they suspended over the coals on forked sticks, regularly fell in the fire. Smoke irritated their eyes, and their backs ached from stooping over their cooking. Rain ruined their bread as they worked in the mud. Then came the tiring job of washing up. Hauling water was a never-ending chore.

Not every place along the trails had firewood for cooking, so women gathered "buffalo chips" to burn instead. After they overcame their initial disgust, they agreed the dried dung made very good fires and smudge pots for repelling mosquitos. Some families facing a long stretch without firewood tied sticks or logs under their wagons as reserve fuel. Others gathered sage and weeds to burn.

Like most pioneer women, Clara probably had only a few clothes, dark in color so they wouldn't show dirt as easily. Washing clothes on the westward journey was a grueling job. Sometimes the wagons had to "lay over" a full day for laundering. If fuel was available, the women heated river or creek water in large kettles. If not, they scrubbed and rinsed clothes in cold water, using harsh soap that chapped their hands. Then they wrung out the wet garments and hung them on bushes or laid them on the grass to dry. By the trip's end, their few dresses were threadbare and showed constant mending. Many emigrant women were embarrassed about their coarse, patched clothing and were hesitant to be seen by visitors along the way. When icy winds struck, they often didn't have enough outer clothes to keep warm. Their woven shawls were no match for the bitter elements.

It is thought that Clara's wagon company may have taken the Smoky Hill Trail from Leavenworth to Denver. This route followed the Kansas and Smoky Hill rivers and then finally crossed one dreaded stretch: the hot, dry, 120-mile expanse between the head of the Smoky Hill River and the Republican River in present-day Colorado. But when the wagons set out in April, 1859, the weather would have been wet and cool, with spring rainstorms pounding down on the travelers. Rivers probably roared with spring runoff, making crossings terrifying and treacherous. Perhaps Clara had shoes to help her endure the cold mud, stones, and thorns under her feet, but perhaps not. Either way, she marched on day after day along the banks of the rain-swollen Kansas River and then up the Smoky Hill Valley, with the hope of finding her daughter, Eliza Jane, in Colorado.

As Clara's wagon train creaked and rattled along, the party would have encountered Native Americans, perhaps Cheyenne or Kiowa. Stories say that Clara felt empathy toward these native peoples whose lifestyle was threatened by the increasing flow of emigrants. She is said to have been part Cherokee herself and to have had a great understanding for people who were in difficulty. Clara insisted that all human beings were God's children.

As the weather turned warmer and then hot, the party would have approached the desertlike expanse between the two rivers. Today we can only imagine how difficult it must have been to cross that desolate area on foot without adequate water or shade. Carrying plenty of full water kegs would make the wagons too heavy for the oxen to pull, so supplies were severely limited. Sometimes, as Clara made herself trudge along, she may have put a piece of dried apple under her tongue to keep her mouth moist. But a long, cool drink of clear water would have to wait.

If Clara's trip was like others on the Smoky Hill route, several days went by—endless, troubled, hot days—before the longed-for shout went up. The Republican River was in sight! They had crossed the worst, most dangerous stretch of trail. Now it was on to the gold camps of Colorado, which in 1859 was still a part of Kansas Territory.

Clara must have seen new graves along the trail—the hard evidence of heartache and suffering in earlier wagon trains. Fatal accidents and disease were common on the overland routes. When a person died, the others wrapped the body in a blanket and buried it beside the trail, usually marking the place with a pile of rocks or a homemade wooden cross.

As the wagons labored their way west, Clara probably yearned for a few minutes of quiet. All day long the cattle bawled. Men shouted instructions. The wagons creaked and groaned as the oxen's heavy hooves pounded the hard ground. Chains clanked and iron wheels clattered over rocks. The canvas wagon covers snapped loudly in the wind.

Clara and the wagon train traveled northwest beyond the Republican River until the breathtaking Rocky Mountains rose in the distance. Clara had never seen anything like them. They stood out against the deep blue sky, white snow glittering on their peaks. She looked forward to reaching the confluence of the South Platte River and Cherry Creek, where chokecherries were said to grow in abundance and the new twin towns of Auraria and Denver nestled. For now, she kept careful watch over the party's food supplies. After nearly eight weeks on the trail, the flour and sugar were probably getting low and the bacon and coffee were almost gone. But Clara somehow continued to feed the men until early June when her party reached the small settlements.

Clara knew the gold camps were crowded with men living in harsh conditions who would gladly pay someone else to wash their clothes for them and she planned to start a laundry service to support herself while she searched for her daughter. Soon after arriving in Denver, though, Clara found a job working in a bakery and a small cabin in which to live. She settled down and began the task for which she is best remembered today: helping to establish Denver's first Sunday School. She gave her time generously to church work, offering the use of her cabin for services. People knew this kind, dedicated newcomer as "Aunt" Clara Brown.

Clara soon realized that a laundry service would be in greater demand in a more remote area. As much as she hated to leave her many new friends, she hired a prospector to take her forty miles up into a rugged mountain mining camp eventually known as Central City. There she settled down and began her laundry work. Historians believe she charged fifty cents (which was commonly paid in gold dust) to wash and iron a shirt. Business was good.

Everywhere she went, she asked about her daughter, but no one seemed to know Eliza Jane's whereabouts. It didn't help that Clara probably did not know her daughter's last name, which might have changed every time Eliza Jane was sold to a new slaveholder. But Clara was not about to give up. She knew a more extensive search—and her many humanitarian projects—would take money. She worked hard and saved her gold dust and bought several buildings in Denver, Central City, and the surrounding settlements. After a few years of careful saving and investing, Clara's holdings were sizeable.

Meanwhile, her Central City cabin became a makeshift hospital and church. She nursed sick or injured miners and contributed time and money to establishing churches in the booming gulch town. Stories say she fed countless hot meals to destitute families by purposely making huge batches of soups or stews and then claiming she had overcooked and needed help using the extra.

After the Civil War ended, Clara knew that Eliza Jane must be free. She decided to go south to search for her, traveling this time by stagecoach and train. Historians believe that although Clara went as far as Kentucky, where her daughter had been sold away from her, she could find no trace of Eliza Jane. Sadly she prepared to return to Central City.

Even in the face of her disappointment, Clara noticed that many of her fellow former slaves in the South were now destitute. Newly freed, their prospects were bleak as they tried to overcome severe prejudice, little formal education, and homelessness. Clara yearned to help. If she could take a group with her to Colorado Territory, she knew she could find good jobs and housing for them. Using the money she had earned through her shrewd investments, she did just that. She paid the way across the plains for a group of men, women, and orphans, some of whom may have been friends or relatives. When they reached Colorado, Clara helped them settle into jobs and homes.

As Clara grew older, her good works continued. When she was in her seventies, old age began to take its toll. It is thought that she developed a heart condition which limited her activities, and that her charitable works had used up most of her money and investments. Several of her buildings had been destroyed by fire. Before long, she was poor and unable to work. But Clara was sure God would care for her. She prayed that He would help find her beloved daughter before her life was over.

It was then that a longtime friend in Denver, where the lower altitude was better for Clara's heart, is believed to have offered her a cottage to live in, cost free, for the rest of her life. Gratefully she accepted and left her Central City home, where she had lived for nineteen years. Soon after, she was named a certified member of the Society of Colorado Pioneers.

Accounts differ on what happened next. Some researchers speculate that in 1882, Clara received a letter from an old friend who had moved to Council Bluffs, Iowa. This friend had met a widow in her early fifties named Mrs. Eliza Jane Brewer who remembered being sold away from her family long ago in Kentucky. After excitedly asking some more questions, the friend felt sure that Mrs. Brewer was Clara's daughter. Clara felt as though she would burst with happiness. She made immediate plans to travel to Iowa by train, hoping her friend was right.

Early in March of 1882, Eliza Jane Brewer met Clara Brown at the Council Bluffs station. According to stories, the two instantly recognized each other and embraced with tears of joy running down their cheeks. After years of searching and wondering, Clara could hardly believe she was reunited with her beloved daughter.

The two enjoyed a long, satisfying visit before Clara returned to Denver where, surrounded by friends, she lived out the last few years of her life. It is believed that Eliza Jane and Eliza's grown daughter joined her there, and were with her when she died on October 23, 1885.

Clara's legacies will always be a part of American history. After her covered wagon trip across the plains, she became one of Colorado's best-loved pioneers, admired for her generosity and compassion. "Aunt" Clara brought the enduring value of selflessness to a primitive wilderness boom town, and is remembered for her genuine love for all human beings. From her humble beginnings, Clara Brown built a memorable life of purpose. ▩

Specific Sources for Clara Brown's Story

Bruyn, Kathleen. *Aunt Clara Brown/ Story of a Black Pioneer*. Boulder, Colorado: Pruett Publishing Company, 1970.

Katz, William Loren. *Black Women of the Old West*. New York: Atheneum Books for Young Readers, 1995.

Pelz, Ruth. *Black Heroes of the Wild West*. Seattle, Washington: Open Hand Publishing, Inc., 1990.

NEAR DEATH
IN THE DESERT

The Story of Sarah Eleanor Bayliss Royce

W hen Sarah Eleanor Bayliss Royce left her eastern Iowa home on April 30, 1849, to cross the continent in a covered wagon, she had no idea how close she and her small family would come to perishing along the way. Their trip began with deep prairie marshes to slow the family's way, and rain to make travel muddy and unpleasant. But Sarah, her husband Josiah, and their only child, two-year-old Mary, were in good spirits as they crept over the plains. They were off to California where gold had been discovered!

To Sarah, sleeping in a wagon seemed strange at first. She had been carefully raised and educated in New York, and had never in her life camped outdoors. But the wagon was cozy, carefully packed with the family's bedding, supplies, and most cherished belongings, including Sarah's Bible and her small lap desk. Their three yoke of oxen and one yoke of cows were strong and healthy, and their provisions were adequate.

It took a month and four days to cross Iowa and reach Council Bluffs on the banks of the Missouri River. This was such a popular "jumping off" place for emigrants traveling west on the overland trails that a whole city of covered wagons was camped along the broad river waiting their turn to ferry across. It wasn't until June 8 that the Royces could transport their wagon and animals to the opposite shore. By then the season was late, and the family was among the last of the travelers to start out.

They spent a day forming a wagon train with others, selecting a captain, adopting rules, and cooking or washing. Then the company turned out onto the Mormon Trail and, as Sarah later wrote in her memoirs, "launched forth upon a journey in which, we all knew, from that hour there was not the least chance of turning back."

Immediately they encountered a group of hundreds of Native Americans who were apprehensive about the newcomers. That year, 1849, the native peoples of the plains had seen more wagon trains than ever before intruding onto their hunting grounds. Deeply disturbed, they began to take action. When the company stopped, they asked the wagon travelers to pay a fee to cross the prairie. But the wagon train leaders had the conflicting idea that the plains belonged to the United States government and that they had the right to cross for free. Arming themselves heavily, the travelers refused the request and started up again. They were allowed to pass peacefully.

As they journeyed on, a man who had joined the company with the Royces became ill, so Sarah and Josiah let him rest in their wagon. Soon he was in intense misery, stretched out behind the seat where Sarah and little Mary rode. Within hours he had died. A doctor from a neighboring wagon train diagnosed cholera, a terrible infectious disease which the pioneers feared because it was often fatal. Sarah and Mary had been thoroughly exposed, and their wagon contaminated. Their fellow travelers kindly helped the Royces disinfect their belongings, washing their bedding and laying their things to dry in the clean air and sun. As the company pushed on, two others fell ill with cholera. In her darkest moments Sarah worried that both she and Josiah might die of cholera and leave their tiny daughter alone among strangers in the wilderness. But Sarah had a strong, unwavering faith in God, and she prayed with all her heart that day. Afterwards, she said that "peace took possession of my soul" and she felt strong again.

The Royce family did stay well, but soon other hardships demanded their attention. They encountered quicksand at a hazardous river crossing and had a difficult time successfully pulling the heavy wagons through it. Next, the wagon train's cattle were spooked by lightning and thunder, and they stampeded. The frantic cattle tipped over two wagons, including the Royce's, splintering three precious wooden wagon wheels. Back East this would be a minor problem, but out on the plains of Nebraska Territory, there was no wood to use for repairs. Again their neighbors came to the rescue, donating hardwood boards they used for a table. The boards were made into the proper parts, and a blacksmith from the wagon train rebuilt the wheels.

On July 9, the party reached Fort Laramie in today's state of Wyoming. Soon afterwards, the Royces and another family chose to leave the wagon train so they could rest on Sundays and travel by themselves. Together they moved on, slowly leaving the plains behind as they climbed into the mountains. They forded rivers, passed famous landmarks like Independence Rock, and at last crossed the South Pass of the Rockies, a beautiful, gentle route over the Continental Divide.

The two families pressed on. Autumn was near, and they could not afford to take the time to choose the longer, safer trails that led to Fort Hall in what is now the state of Idaho. These routes bypassed the dangerous desert country west of the Great Salt Lake. Instead, they struggled across the dusty plateaus to the south, where the water and even the grass were poisoned with alkali, and through the wild

UNIDENTIFIED WAGON TRAIN TRAVELERS ON THE MORMON TRAIL

Wasatch Mountains. The Great Salt Lake in today's state of Utah appeared over a rise on August 18, 1849, and they gratefully descended into Salt Lake City.

There the Royces replenished their supplies. Time was short as they loaded the wagon with just enough provisions to travel across the desert country and the Sierra Nevadas to the west. Anything more would make the wagon too heavy for the tired oxen and would slow their progress.

An elderly man who also wanted to go to California asked if he could travel with the family, and a few days later a couple of young men wanted to join them also. Glad for the company, Sarah and Josiah agreed. It wasn't long, though, before the young men's provisions began running out. They asked to share the Royce's carefully measured flour, promising to hunt for meat in return. The family again agreed. But hunting in such arid country was often unsuccessful, and food began to dwindle.

For days they inched across the sunbaked land west of the Great Salt Lake. Ahead lay a feared forty-mile-wide desert. Sarah and Josiah had a sketchy instruction sheet for crossing this vast desolate stretch, but they received more specific directions from a party of pioneers who were returning from California along the same route. The leader of the eastbound travelers drew a map in the sand with a stick. The Royces were to push ahead until they reached the "sink"—a place where a river runs underground—in the Humboldt River. Soon after, they were to turn left and follow a rough trail for two or three miles. This led to grassy meadows with plenty of good water. He advised them to camp in the meadows for a few days to let the cattle rest, and in the meanwhile, cut and dry as much hay as the wagon could hold and fill every container with water. Then they should start out across the forty-mile-wide desert, stopping now and then to eat, drink, and rest. Traveling this way, they could cross the scorching expanse in about twenty-four hours.

With this new information, Sarah, Josiah, Mary, and their companions moved ahead. Unknown to them, the guide sheet they had brought from Salt Lake City was incorrect, indicating that the sink of the Humboldt was ten miles beyond its actual location. Traveling by moonlight with these faulty directions, the party missed the turnoff to the grassy meadows before they even began looking for it.

They traveled the whole day across the baking desert sand, expecting at any moment to come upon the road to the meadows. By evening, the dreadful reality became clear: they had missed the fork in the road much earlier and were "now miles out on the desert without a mouthful of food for the cattle and only two or three quarts of water in a little cask." Sarah watched anxiously as the oxen's heads drooped lower and lower to the ground. She knew in her heart they could not pull the wagon much farther without hay, rest, and water. She, Josiah, and the others were weary, frightened, and thirsty. They decided to stop for the night where they were.

In the morning, a life-or-death decision had to be made. The meadows with their life-giving grass and water must be twelve to fifteen miles behind them. Would it be better to try to finish crossing the desert or to go back and find the meadows? Everyone but little Mary, who kept asking for a drink, knew that they would die on the parched sand if they made the wrong choice. And they knew the oxen desperately needed food in order to pull the wagon to safety in either direction. It was then they remembered that their mattresses were stuffed with hay! There wasn't much, but perhaps by offering the oxen a few mouthfuls along the way, it would be enough to save the animals from death.

The desert stretched to the horizon as they despairingly turned around and started back. Each mile seemed to go on forever, and every footstep was harder than the last. Sarah wrote in her memoirs:

Turn back! What a chill the words sent through one. *Turn back,* on a journey like that; in which every mile had been gained by most earnest labor . . . In all that long journey no steps ever seemed so heavy, so hard to take, as those with which I turned my back to the sun that afternoon of October 4th, 1849.

Partway back, they saw another small party coming toward them. Their hope was renewed: perhaps these travelers would have enough feed and water to share. But the other party, although kind and concerned, could not spare their supplies without endangering their own lives. They told the Royces exactly where to find the meadows. To the Royces' dismay, it was at least fourteen to sixteen miles farther.

Sarah, tired and thirsty though she was, began to walk instead of ride in the wagon to lighten the load on the oxen. She vowed to drink very little of the sparse water, giving her portion instead to Mary or to some of the others. At times, she lagged far behind the wagon as it lumbered back across the hot, dry sand. Mile after slow mile inched by as the terrible day wore on. Darkness came, and once again the party stopped.

The next morning, the oxen ate the last meager mouthful of hay from the mattresses. The water was nearly gone and the day was growing hotter. Again Mary begged for a drink. Sarah knew her little girl could not last long if their water gave out. As the oxen's heads drooped nearly to the ground, Sarah prayed fervently. She made herself walk on asking God to help them, and not to let Mary die. Suddenly she heard whoops of joy ahead, and the jubilant cry, "Grass and water!" They had reached the meadows!

Sarah would never forget her overwhelming gratitude at the sight of the welcome oasis. The party rested and refreshed themselves, and then set to work cutting and drying hay, cooking, and collecting water for the desert crossing.

A couple of days later, with the wagon fully loaded, they set out again. Because of their careful preparations, the journey was hard but successful. They pushed across the dry sand all the way to the tree-lined Carson River on the other side. Now only the high, snow-capped Sierra Nevadas blocked their way to California. But it was October, and snow storms swirled through the high elevations. Approaching the foothills, Sarah and Josiah were concerned about making it over the steep passes with winter setting in. Still, there was no choice: they had to attempt to cross.

As they neared the foothills, a small cloud of dust appeared in the distance. When it came closer, the family could see two men on horseback, each leading a mule. With their loose clothing flying behind them like wings, they galloped down a steep slope directly toward the Royces. Sarah, well aware of the party's dangerous mountain crossing ahead, thought the riders looked as though they had been sent from heaven.

She and Josiah were shocked when the men said they were searching for the Royces. The riders turned out to be United States government agents sent out to help late emigrants over the formidable mountain passes. They had been told about Sarah and Josiah by the wagon travelers who hadn't been able to share their supplies in the desert. Sarah wished she could thank the concerned woman in the party who had insisted the rescue workers try to help them. Instead she said a prayer of deep gratitude.

The skillful government agents helped the family pack their most important belongings, for they had to leave the wagon behind and finish the journey on mules and on foot. And they had to hurry, because although the weather had cleared for a short time, more winter storms were coming. In a few days, mountain blizzards would make the trail impassable. So it was settled that Sarah and Mary would ride on one of the government mules, and the other animals, including the Royce's oxen, would carry the party's food and most valuable belongings. Sarah selected, among her other essentials, her Bible, her tiny lap desk, and a book of John Milton's classical writings. Then they gave a last look at their faithful wagon, and with specific directions from the government agents, said their heartfelt thanks and started over the mountains.

After two long days of vertical rocky trails strewn with huge boulders and cold nights when their water turned to ice, they stood at the summit overlooking California's Sacramento Valley. Sarah looked down onto the warm welcoming land below and knew that she had found her new home. She wrote in her memoirs: "California, land of sunny skies—that was my first look into your smiling face. I loved you from that moment, for you seemed to welcome me with loving look into rest and safety."

The family descended into the mining camps, which were scattered throughout the Sierra Nevada foothills, and set up their tent just days before the mountains were snowed in. They stayed for about two months before moving on to Sacramento, then San Francisco, and finally back to the gold camps.

Over the years, the Royces made their living by farming and selling groceries to the miners in the crude tent cities. Often their home was a sturdy, portable canvas house. As time went by, two more daughters and a son were born to Sarah and Josiah. Sarah herself gave them their early schooling. Their youngest child, Josiah, with a solid education from his mother, grew up to be one of America's foremost philosophers. Later in his life, Josiah asked his mother to write the story of her westward journey and her years in early California.

Sarah is remembered as a refined, educated woman who gave up the cultured things she loved to take a harrowing journey west in a rustic wagon. Despite the rowdy lawlessness of early California, she never allowed herself or her children to lose sight of the refinements of civilization: the libraries, schools, and churches which she, and others like her, helped bring to the mining camps of the Gold Rush. ▣

Specific Sources for Sarah Eleanor Bayliss Royce's Story

Editors of Time-Life Books with text by Joan Swallow Reiter. The Old West Books. *The Women*. New York: Time-Life Books, 1979.

Levy, Joann. *They Saw the Elephant/Women in the California Gold Rush*. Hamden, Connecticut: Archon Books, an imprint of The Shoe String Press, 1990.

National Geographic Society. *Trails West*. Washington, D.C.: National Geographic Society, Special Publications Division, 1979.

Royce, Sarah. *A Frontier Lady/Recollections of the Gold Rush and Early California*. Lincoln and London: University of Nebraska Press, 1977. (Reprint of the 1932 edition by Yale University Press.)

WITH DETERMINED OPTIMISM

The Story of Sarah Raymond

Twenty-five-year-old Sarah Raymond rode to the top of a green bluff on her bay pony. She could see the small group of covered wagons below, making their slow way west across the vast Iowa plains. Holding her sunbonnet in her hand, she waved merrily to her friends and family.

From her viewpoint, Sarah could watch the two wagons she shared with her mother and grown brothers that summer of 1865. Her father had died several years before. There was a large, heavy wagon to haul household goods, and a lighter spring-wagon to carry everyday items and to provide a sleeping place for Sarah and Mrs. Raymond. She could even see their churn filled with this morning's heavy cream fastened to the front of the freight wagon. The wagon's steady lurching throughout the day would turn the cream into soft butter in time for the family to enjoy it on their homemade bread for supper.

Sarah could also see the four wagons belonging to the large Kerfoot family, her neighbors from back home in Sand Hill, Missouri. Sarah's gentle friend Neelie would be riding in one, perhaps mending clothes for her younger sisters and brothers. What a sweet, helpful person she was, and how Sarah valued her friendship. Sarah had been trying to teach Neelie how to cook over a campfire. But preparing food for a family of twelve was no easy task, even for an experienced cook. And the Kerfoot women were not experienced. At home, servants had always prepared the meals. Neelie's biscuits were hard and dry, but she cheerfully kept trying to learn the art of baking in a sheet iron camp stove. And she doggedly brought the refinements of home to the trail by polishing the family's tin dishes until they gleamed, and making sure she put out a bouquet of flowers with the evening meal.

Sarah urged her pony down from the bluff and hurried to catch up to the passing wagons. She wasn't afraid of riding alone in this wild country and often took solitary rides for recreation. She had a strong faith that God would watch over and protect her. Her mother, though, was concerned about the many dangers surrounding them and preferred that Sarah stay near the group.

In Sarah's mind, it had been a glorious trip so far. Her buoyant spirits could not be dampened by cold rain, mud, or even swarms of biting gnats and mosquitoes. She happily told friends, ". . . it is so jolly to be going across the continent; it is like a picnic every day for months; I was always sorry picnic days were so short, and now it will be an all Summer picnic." Her cheerfulness brought joy to an otherwise serious journey. When the young men of the train hung a homemade swing from a low-hanging tree limb, Sarah (or "Miss Sallie" as she was sometimes fondly nicknamed) was the first to soar high into the leafy branches. Although she was careful to help her mother with the trail work, she also took time to climb nearby landmarks for spectacular vistas, or appreciate the beauty of an approaching storm. She regularly visited her friends, especially Neelie. Later she would be glad she had.

Before leaving Missouri on May 1, 1865, Sarah promised friends she would keep a journal of her trip west, so she carefully recorded

SARAH RAYMOND
MONTANA HISTORICAL SOCIETY, HELENA

each day's events in her diary. Her wagon train friends teased her gently about this, but her mother felt Sarah's writing was a gift to be nurtured. Mrs. Raymond willingly did much of the evening work so Sarah would have time to record their trip. Many years after their westward journey was over, Sarah's diary was published.

By the mid-1860s, when Sarah and her family were traveling, relations between the white travelers and Native Americans had become explosive. Often there were conflicts which resulted in deaths along the trails. The U.S. government had established new military posts on the western routes and requested that emigrants travel in groups of forty to sixty wagons for protection. Wagon trains were to camp near each other if possible. To obey these new orders, the Raymonds' small group joined a much larger wagon train in Nebraska soon after crossing the Missouri River. The Hardinbrooke Train, as it was called, would stay together until the group had passed through today's Colorado and most of Wyoming. In spite of the fear and hostility that existed between the travelers and Native Americans— discussed openly even in Sarah's diary—there were no violent encounters on the Raymonds' trip, although they saw grisly evidence of several conflicts. Nevertheless, each night the wagon train formed a tight circle and corralled the animals inside. Men took turns guarding the camp, and the Raymonds' watchdog, Caesar, slept under their wagon. The group traveled close to other large trains.

As the wagons snaked across the wide prairie, it became clear that Sarah was well liked by everyone. Time after time she offered her help when someone was sick or trail-weary. She nursed fellow travelers, babysat a child whose mother was ill, drove the horse team that pulled the spring-wagon, and comforted those who were discouraged. She was generous in sharing her sleek pony with her friends and family after she realized that jolting along in a hard wagon all day was exhausting.

The unmarried gentlemen did not fail to notice Sarah's thoughtful and sunny nature. Many times, one young man or another asked to walk with her in the moonlight or accompany her on a horseback ride. They gave her candy, bouquets of wildflowers, and sweet red apples. Sarah appreciated the gifts and friendship very much, but seemed in no hurry to become attached. She was independent and self-sufficient. After all, she had earned her teaching certificate at the age of fourteen—something that was possible for a diligent student at that time—and had already taught school for several years.

Mrs. Raymond, Sarah, and her two brothers, eighteen-year-old Winthrop, and twenty-year-old Hillhouse, soon faced a decision which would influence the rest of their lives. When they left Missouri, they hadn't decided upon a final destination. California's sunny winters beckoned to the Raymonds, but so did Oregon's lush valleys and the gold discoveries in Montana Territory. Finally they chose Montana, and turned their thoughts to the well-known gold camp of Virginia City. Sarah hoped they could persuade Neelie's family to join them, but feared the Kerfoots would choose to settle in California instead.

Sarah was surprised at how many people were going west that year. But the bitter Civil War had just ended. Southerners and Northerners alike were weary and heavy-hearted: many were ready for a new life in a new place. On July 1, the party reached Colorado's South Platte River along with neighboring wagon trains. Sarah drove the horse team and spring-wagon across the half-mile-wide ford. The next day, as her group camped with others on the north bank of the river, she marveled at the great number of wagons, animals, and people (about one thousand), and at the temporary city of tents that sprang up overnight.

Although the wagons were able to ford the South Platte, by 1865 westward travelers were sometimes forced to cross shaky toll bridges. The bridge keepers would block off easy fording places with large logs or ditches, so there was no choice but to cross the bridge and pay the toll, usually fifty cents or a dollar per wagon. Sarah reported with exasperation many such bridges on their trip.

On July 4, the dusty wagons stopped for a few hours in a shady grove of cottonwoods. To celebrate the holiday, the families ate savory roast antelope with oyster dressing and even cake and custard, carefully made with the last of the fresh eggs they had preserved in salt.

Sarah's diary tells of picking native gooseberries and gathering wild onions. Perhaps she, like some pioneer women, rolled out a pie crust on the wagon seat and baked a gooseberry pie over glowing coals. One hot afternoon near Elk Mountain, Sarah's brother found a small patch of sheltered snow, and Sarah took delight in eating a snowball. Another day she wrote about watching a prairie dog colony. In the evenings, she and her friends gathered, probably around a crackling campfire, for guitar music and singing.

Near the crossing of the North Platte River in today's Wyoming, a note of anxiety crept into Sarah's writing. Neelie was sick. Sarah wrote: "Neelie continues to drag around; she will not acknowledge that she is sick enough to go to bed, but she certainly looks sick . . ."

Neelie had good days and bad. Sometimes she felt better, but other times she was feverish and weak. Finally in late July, she came to Sarah for help. Sarah wrote:

. . . I was sitting in mother's camp-chair idling and thinking, when Neelie came to me. She dropped upon the grass beside me and, laying her head in my lap, said, "Oh, Miss Sallie, I am afraid I am going to be sick in spite of everything, and I have tried so hard to get well without sending for the doctor."

The wagon company was fortunate to have with them Dr. Fletcher, a young physician who had taken a liking to Neelie. Sarah helped put the sick girl to bed and then called for him, knowing he would offer Neelie his best care and prescribe whatever medication he could.

The group pressed on. Each bump and hollow jostled Neelie as she lay in her bed. Sarah, riding her pony nearby, wondered if the Kerfoot family's poor, monotonous diet had made Neelie sick. But Dr. Fletcher and another physician, Dr. Howard, who was soon called from a neighboring wagon train, agreed that she had mountain fever. This was most likely typhoid, a serious contagious illness that causes, among other symptoms, high fever, headache, and stiff muscles. The doctors agreed Neelie might get better if the Kerfoot family stopped for a few days to allow her to rest. But as much as the family loved their sweet, unselfish daughter, her father was afraid of the dangers facing a lone, isolated family, and decided it was best to keep up with the rest of the train. They continued along the grueling trail. Sarah stayed beside her friend, giving her the doctors' medicines and watching over her at the risk of catching mountain fever herself. Even with Sarah's tender care, however, Neelie continued to get worse.

Mr. Kerfoot had made a firm decision to settle in California. Up ahead, Sarah knew, was the split in the road where the wagons bound for Montana Territory and those heading to California would have to part company. She dreaded the day when she would have to leave her friend.

On July 27, the wagon train divided into two parts in preparation for the fork in the trail. As she watched the Kerfoot wagons join the California-bound company, Sarah took comfort in the fact that for the next few days, until they reached the fork, the two parties would travel near each other. She was sure she would see her friend again.

On Saturday, August 5, Neelie's cousin Frank from the California train galloped up to Sarah's party and asked Dr. Fletcher to come see the sick girl immediately. Sarah followed, hoping to see her too. She listened intently when Frank described Neelie as "delirious" and "too weak to talk." When they arrived at the Kerfoot wagon train, Sarah was profoundly disappointed. The doctor felt any excitement at all might make Neelie worse. It was decided that her joy at seeing Sarah would excite her too much. Sadly, Sarah agreed and returned to her own wagon train.

All too soon, the Raymond's party turned north to Montana Territory. Sarah wrote these heart-wrenching lines in her diary: "I feel the parting with our friends so distressingly. It is not likely we will meet again in this life." Each day in her prayers she remembered her friend traveling in pain and fever along the rough trail to California, and almost certainly must have asked the family to write her in Virginia City about Neelie's health.

Sarah felt it was her duty to stay cheerful. As saddened as she was by recent events, she kept up her brave attitude while the small group wound its way north through rugged Idaho. She reported curing a sick oxen by feeding him melted lard and bacon, meeting a spunky ninety-three-year-old woman traveling with another wagon party, tracking down a stolen horse, and taking long rides on her pony. They followed steep mountain trails, causing Sarah to wonder if the wagons "would turn a somersault" coming down. Some days they went fishing and ate their plentiful catch for breakfast.

Sarah continued to worry quietly about Neelie, but another concern bothered her, too. The Raymonds had used up much of their money on the trip west replenishing supplies and paying tolls. They would need more once they reached Virginia City. Several people had offered to buy her well-fed, healthy pony, but she had always refused. Now, as they neared their destination, she felt that, agonizing as it would be, she ought to sell him to help her family. Unwilling to do it herself, she asked her brother Hillhouse to accept a generous offer of $125 in gold dust. After the gentle pony was gone, Sarah couldn't stop her tears.

On September 1, the party entered what is now Montana. When Sarah awoke the next morning and peeked out of the wagon, soft snow glimmered on the surrounding mountains. A few days later, on September 5, Mrs. Raymond, Sarah, Winthrop, and Hillhouse arrived at their destination: the dirty, bustling mining town of Virginia City. Sarah wrote: "It is the shabbiest town I ever saw, not a really good house in it. Hillhouse and I, after hunting up and down the two most respectable looking streets, found a log cabin with two rooms that we rented for eight dollars per month." Letters were waiting for them at the post office. One was from Neelie's cousin, Frank.

Sarah's heart must have faltered when she saw it, for the letter contained the bad news she had feared: Neelie had died. Shortly after the wagons had separated, and after a long, hot, dusty day of traveling, Neelie had fallen into what her father thought was peaceful sleep. But although every effort was made, no one could wake her, and the next morning she took her last breath. From her faraway new home in the muddy gold camp, Sarah grieved deeply.

For the first time during her long journey, she wrote in her journal about being homesick. But with her typical fortitude she set to work to make the best of the situation, cleaning the cabin—which had a dirt roof—and trying to overcome her sadness about Neelie. To earn some money, she took in sewing. It wasn't long before she found a job as Virginia City's schoolteacher.

Teaching in the primitive town was not easy: Sarah had schoolchildren of all ages, as well as an odd assortment of textbooks that had been brought to the gold camp by one family or another. With these meager supplies, she patiently set to work to teach her young students to read and write.

Sarah probably taught in Virginia City for just one year, because on May 27, 1867, she married thirty-four-year-old James M. Herndon, a carpenter and miner who later operated a furniture store in Virginia City. Sarah became a homemaker and Sunday School teacher. She and James eventually had five children, and the family spent many years together in Montana.

Sarah Raymond Herndon always remembered her four-month-long covered wagon trip to Montana Territory. Her journey was made remarkable by her cheerful, courageous outlook in the face of hardship and illness. With determined optimism, she brightened her fellow travelers' darkest moments, and made the difficult trip seem more like the summer picnic she imagined than the desolate journey many other covered wagon travelers experienced. ▣

Specific Sources for Sarah Raymond's Story

Griffith, H. Winter, M.D. *Complete Guide to Symptoms, Illness, & Surgery*. Tucson, Arizona: Body Press, a division of HPBooks, Inc., 1985.

Raymond, Sarah. *Days on the Road/Crossing the Plains in 1865*. New York: Burr Printing House, 1902.

Settle, Raymond W. and Mary Lund, editors. *Overland Days to Montana in 1865/The Diary of Sarah Raymond and Journal of Dr. Waid Howard*. Glendale, California: The Arthur H. Clark Company, 1971.

World Book Encyclopedia. World Book, Inc. Chicago, London, Sydney, Toronto, 1990.

GRANDMOTHER ON HORSEBACK
The Story of Tabitha Moffatt Brown

Grandma Tabitha Moffatt Brown climbed down from her tall horse and glanced anxiously at her companion. Mounted precariously in his saddle, seventy-seven-year-old Captain John Brown, her brother-in-law, was ready to collapse from fatigue and hunger. Tabitha looked at the rugged, mountainous wilderness surrounding the remote wagon trail over which they had just ridden. What could she do? Her tired, aching body cried out for food and a soft bed. Darkness was coming, and it was raining. Captain Brown was so sick and worn out she wondered if he would live through the night. They had no shelter from the wind and rain, and only three strips of bacon left.

Thoughts of ever present wolves and of the cold, wet night ahead without a fire made her shiver. Quickly she said a prayer for their safety, and for the safety of her loved ones back down the trail with their covered wagons: her daughter Pherne, Pherne's husband Virgil Pringle, and their five children. Their food was gone and their few remaining cattle were so weak they could not move on without rest. Pherne and Virgil had insisted that Tabitha and the frail Captain Brown leave the hungry wagon travelers and ride ahead on horseback.

Perhaps the two of them could catch the emigrants in the covered wagons who had passed the day before. Tabitha hoped the group ahead had enough provisions to share.

Now, at nightfall in the mountains, she squared her small shoulders and took a deep breath. She had promised herself she'd never cry on her trip west to Oregon. So far she hadn't, even when she had to abandon her battered covered wagon and most of her belongings back on the trail. She wasn't about to start now. Briskly, she took the saddle and saddlebags off her wet horse and found her wagon sheet.

"What are you going to do?" asked Captain Brown, his voice weak.

"I am going to camp for the night," Tabitha answered.

The thought of spending the night under such circumstances was too much for the elderly man. He moaned and fell from his horse. Swiftly Tabitha threw the wagon sheet over a tree limb so it formed a makeshift tent. She unsaddled and tied the captain's horse and helped the old gentleman into the tent, covering him with blankets. Then she, too, crouched under the shelter, asking God to watch over them.

Many long hours later, a faint glow in the east told Tabitha their treacherous night was over. She later remembered that welcome morning in a letter to her brother and sister. She wrote:

As soon as light had dawned, I pulled down my tent, saddled the horses; found the Captain so as to stand upon his feet— just at this moment one of the emigrants that I was trying to overtake came to me—he was in search of venison—half a mile ahead were the wagons I was trying to catch up with. We were soon there, and ate plentifully of fresh venison.

Tabitha, who was a tiny sixty-six-year-old widow and a former schoolteacher, and two of her three grown children with their families

TABITHA MOFFATT BROWN
PACIFIC UNIVERSITY ARCHIVES, FOREST GROVE, OREGON

had left Missouri in April of 1846. Tabitha's oldest son Orus, who with his wife Lavina had eight children, was appointed pilot for a wagon train that traveled six days ahead of Tabitha's. She and Captain Brown, and the Pringles with their children, among others, followed.

It was a "pleasing and prosperous" trip, Tabitha later wrote, all the way from Missouri to Fort Hall in today's southern Idaho. But they still had eight hundred miles to go and already it was August. Travel would be almost impossible after the snows began. Beyond Fort Hall, a "rascally fellow who came out from the settlement in Oregon" assured Tabitha's party he had found a shortcut to the Willamette Valley. He persuaded them to follow him, and promised he would get them to the valley long before those who took the better-established route—the one that Tabitha's oldest son Orus and his family had taken—down the Columbia River valley.

Some of the weary travelers, including Tabitha, Captain Brown, and Pherne and Virgil Pringle, decided to try the new route, which became known as the Applegate Trail. Too late, the travelers found out the rough shortcut was not yet suited for covered wagons. Worse, it carried them far south of Oregon into Utah Territory and California. Tabitha wrote briefly about the hardships and suffering they endured: a long bleak desert to cross, wagons that broke, and weary oxen that gave out. She watched her fellow travelers start to starve. Some even died.

But it was in Oregon's Umpqua Mountains that the real trouble set in. Tabitha wrote that her family was the first of their group to start into the twelve-mile canyon. Of the hundreds of wagons that tried to make it through, only one made it without breaking apart. She said the canyon was "strewn with dead cattle, broken wagons, beds, clothing, and everything but provisions of which we were nearly destitute." It was in this canyon that Tabitha and Captain Brown were urged to leave the group and ride for safety. Once they caught up with the emigrants ahead and feasted on venison, they traveled on and in a few days arrived at the base of another block of mountains. There, while Tabitha and Captain Brown waited for a road to be cut, the Pringle family caught up with them. Tabitha wrote:

> . . . Here we were obliged to wait for more emigrants to help cut a road through; here my children and grandchildren came up with us—a joyful meeting. They had been near starving. Mr. Pringle tried to shoot a wolf, but he was too weak and trembling to hold his rifle steady.

Winter set in. The party struggled through the cold, snowy mountains, sometimes advancing only a mile or two each day. After a week their food was gone again. Virgil Pringle left the stalled party and set off on horseback for the settlements to bring supplies to his family. No one knew if he would be successful or even if he would return.

Meanwhile, Tabitha's son Orus and his large family had reached the Oregon settlements by way of the better-traveled route. Word reached him of the life-threatening hardships being encountered by the Applegate Trail travelers. Deeply concerned for his mother and his sister's family, he loaded four packhorses with provisions and set off to find them.

Somewhere along the route, Orus met Virgil Pringle riding for help. The two men soon arrived at the camp of the starving travelers. Tabitha described that joyful night in her letters.

> We had all retired to rest in our tents, hoping to forget our troubles until daylight should remind us of our sad fate. In the gloomy stillness of the night, hoofbeats of horses were heard rushing to our tents—directly a halloo—it was the well-known

voice of Orus Brown and Virgil Pringle; who can realize the joy?

Pushing on once again, the thin, tired travelers finally reached the settlements in Oregon's Willamette Valley. On Christmas Day 1846, Tabitha entered a house for the first time in nine months. It was the home of a Methodist minister in Salem. He asked Tabitha to care for his family and house through the winter. She traded her housekeeping services for room and board for both herself and Captain Brown.

During the final leg of her journey, Tabitha had noticed a small lump in the finger of her glove. Now that she was settled, she turned her glove inside out to look more closely. A little coin worth about six cents—a picayune—fell into her hand. It was all the money she had to begin her new life in Oregon. With it, she purchased three needles. Then she traded a few of her old clothes for some buckskin and began making and selling gloves.

As the months went by, Tabitha became concerned about the children in the settlements whose parents had died on the overland trails. She realized these children, and a few of the surrounding Native American children, desperately needed a home where they could go to school and grow up. Two missionaries originally from Vermont, Reverend Harvey and Emeline Clark, and another minister, Reverend George Atkinson, gave their support. In the spring of 1848, they arranged for an old log meeting house to become Tabitha's home where she could "receive all poor children and be a mother to them." The Clarks and others agreed to help provide furnishings and provisions: "The neighbors had collected together what broken knives and forks, tin pans and dishes they could part with for the Oregon Pioneer to commence housekeeping. A well educated lady from the east, a missionary's wife, was the teacher."

By summer, Tabitha had thirty boarders ranging in age from four to twenty-one. The amount of work was staggering, but with her typical energy, Tabitha tackled the job. She told of mixing 3,423 pounds of flour with her own hands in order to feed her hungry guests. At one point, she planted a garden and served red, ripe Oregon strawberries to the children for dessert. She was in charge of the boarding house and school, which became known as the Tualatin Academy. Trustees, including both Reverend Clark and Reverend Atkinson, were selected to plan for the future.

As the Tualatin Academy grew and prospered, the trustees began thinking about establishing a university. With this in mind, Reverend Clark donated a piece of land, and a large new building was constructed on it. The Academy's charter was then amended to include a "collegiate department" called Pacific University.

Today, Tabitha's name is inscribed in the Oregon State Capitol as a prominent early citizen. In 1987, the state legislature named her the "Mother of Oregon." Thanks in part to her generosity and hard work, the modern campus of Pacific University stands solidly amid towering oaks, its many faculty members educating students from all over the world. In the university's Old College Hall, which was built in 1850, is a small museum that displays some of Tabitha Moffatt Brown's belongings: her wedding ring, a school bell, a black lace cap, a letter written in her beautiful script. Hanging above it all is an unassuming portrait of Grandma Brown, who with her clear, intelligent eyes still seems to oversee the school and its students. ▨

Specific Sources for Tabitha Moffatt Brown's Story

Brown, Tabitha Moffatt. The "Brimfield Heroine" letter, August 1854, as published in *Covered Wagon Women/ Diaries and Letters from the Western Trails 1840 -1890*, volume 1, edited and compiled by Kenneth L. Holmes. Glendale, California: Arthur H. Clarke, 1983.

Pringle, Virgil K. "Journal of Virgil K. Pringle: Crossing the Plains in 1846." Manuscript copy. Pacific University Archives, Harvey W. Scott Memorial Library, Forest Grove, Oregon.

Read, Richard T. "The Early Days of Pacific University." Pacific University, Forest Grove, Oregon.

Spooner, Ella Brown. *Tabitha Brown's Western Adventures*. New York: Exposition Press, 1958.

CHILLING
JOURNEY

The Story of Mary Rockwood Powers

Mary Rockwood Powers watched her husband, Dr. Americus Powers, lead their tired horses through a hip-deep stream. Who was this man she had married? The westward journey had turned him into someone she hardly knew. He had once been a considerate husband, but was now sullen, angry, and unpredictable. How would she and her three young children ever reach California if he kept behaving so strangely? And what about their poor horses that were so worn out they wobbled in the harness as they pulled the heavy covered wagon?

Fort Laramie was just ahead. After days of travel on the Old Mormon Trail that spring of 1856, Mary was eager to reach the fort because her husband had promised to trade the weak horses for some sturdy oxen there. She hoped they could make it that far. To make the time go faster, Mary quietly prayed and read *Pilgrim's Progress* to her children, Sarah, Cephas, and Celia. She wrote long letters to her mother and sisters back home and kept a diary.

Mary's devotion to her children was clear. She loved them deeply and cared for them with all her energy. When a cold hailstorm thundered down one dark, windy night on the unsheltered plains, she protected them by crouching in the wagon and holding a blanket over the front opening. After the two-hour storm was over, Mary was soaked with icy water and was so stiff her husband had to help her move. The children still slept, safely nestled in their blankets.

Already it seemed as if they had been on the road forever. An acquaintance had borrowed their precious rifle and never returned it, leaving the Powerses with no way to hunt or protect themselves. Mary had lost track of the days. Worse than that, the wagon train they had joined left them behind "to get along the best we could." Mary wrote that it was because the exhausted horses couldn't keep up, but it was highly unusual for a company to abandon one of its families. Researchers speculate that perhaps Dr. Powers's erratic, moody behavior caused the split.

From Mary's descriptive writings it is plain that the journey had been hard on him. At one point on the trip, she wrote that he had "grown so peculiar" and that "For some days the Doctor had been falling into his old sullen mood again; out of humor with everyone, and the more kindness anyone showed us the worse he got." Dr. Powers avoided others, sometimes not speaking to them unless it was to argue. He refused to ask for help even when his family was in danger. At one point along the trail, he drove off, leaving behind a sick child who badly needed his care.

It was obvious that the doctor's decision to buy beautiful, expensive horses to pull the family across the overland trail was a mistake. The wagon weighed nine hundred pounds when empty; filled with the Powerses' household goods and their provisions, it was far too heavy for fine horses, even on flat, dry stretches. Steep, rocky, muddy parts of the trail wore the animals to the bone. But Mary bit her tongue. Beautiful, educated, and restrained, she—like many other women of the time—felt her husband was the head of the family. Her duty, she believed, was to accept his decisions and be a supportive helpmate.

She was to care for her children, prepare the meals, take care of the domestic chores, and try to make the journey as pleasant as possible.

But after Dr. Powers passed Fort Laramie and then the next fort without trading for oxen or buying flour, Mary was paralyzed with fear. Had her husband lost his mind? The family was nearly out of food, having fed some of their flour to the horses for strength. She was terrified to enter the Black Hills without supplies or reliable oxen. Again and again, the doctor promised to take care of the problems, but each time he failed to act. Day after day he hitched the half-dead horses to the wagon.

His odd ways frightened and puzzled Mary, but true to her upbringing and the customs of the time, she held back her comments. It was only in her letters to her mother and sisters that she poured out her heart, saying she feared she was traveling with "a maniac." "I felt as though myself and little ones were at the mercy of a mad man. It did not seem that any man in his right mind would take the course the Doctor was taking. I said nothing but thought the more."

On and on the family struggled. Dr. Powers had to alternate their spent horses every few hundred yards to let them rest. The animals foamed at the mouth, and were so stiff and worn out they could hardly stand. One leaned against another for support. Sometimes they collapsed in the harness. Mary ached for them, and would gladly have walked all the way to California to save them her weight in the wagon, but she was expected to drive the team.

Up and down hills, through ravines, and across streams they traveled, bumping over rocks and going, as Mary put it, "inch by inch at a time." Finally it became plain that she had to take matters into her own hands. She told her husband that if he failed to trade for oxen at the next opportunity, then she would. They had come upon an emigrant party, and the doctor again promised he would make arrangements in the morning.

MARY ROCKWOOD POWERS AND DR. AMERICUS W. POWERS
REPRINTED FROM *SOME ANNALS OF THE POWERS FAMILY.*

The next day Dr. Powers did ask to trade, but he waited until it was too late. The emigrants needed to get on the road, so they were reluctant to take time to trade. Gathering her courage, Mary spoke to the leader, Mr. Hendrick, herself. He assured her that if the family could travel with their own horses one more day, his party would lend the Powerses some oxen that evening. That day, one of the horses nearly died. The remaining horses slowly dragged the clumsy wagon over the hills, but finally made it to camp. True to his word, Mr. Hendrick let the Powerses borrow three teams of oxen. Several families offered them dried apples, beans, and fresh game or fish. Gratefully, Mary accepted. By then she and the doctor had only three dollars left.

To Mary's horror, it wasn't long before Dr. Powers had a disagreement with the others in the train. Harsh words were exchanged, and the doctor broke away from the party. (Gentle, refined Mary wrote in her diary, "I forbear giving the details.") The wagon train women kindly shared gifts with Mary, who already had become their respected friend, and said goodbye with "tears running down their sunburnt cheeks." Mary reported that the men were so concerned for her that they, too, shed tears. Once again, after returning the borrowed oxen, the little family went on alone.

Fortunately they were only several days from the settlements at Salt Lake, but by then two of the horses had died and the others were back in the harness again. Laboring on step by step, so worn they could "hardly crawl," Mary wrote, the animals brought the wagon to a creek with steep banks. They got the wagon down into the creek bed but could not pull it up the other side. Dr. Powers and Mary unloaded the children and their belongings, and unhitched the horses. They led the animals to the top of the bank where the footing was better, and tied them to the wagon with a long rope. Mary was instructed to hold up the wagon tongue and then quickly jump aside as the horses pulled the wagon up the incline.

Something went wrong. The heavy wagon started up the steep bank, but before Mary could spring out of the way, it slipped back down. Its huge iron-rimmed wheels ran over her ankle. Thanks to the softness of the gravel underfoot, Mary's ankle was painful and badly bruised but not broken. The family pushed on.

Finally they arrived at the Mormon settlements near Salt Lake, where they rested for several days and tended their horses. The Mormon settlers invited the Powerses to stay with them, gave them food and desperately needed supplies, and allowed them to graze the horses. Mary returned their generosity as best she could, sharing thread, stockings, and coffee. She traded two white blankets for two hundred pounds of flour. By mid-August the horses were ready to move on.

It was then an incident occurred that had devastating effects on Mary. One afternoon, the family reached a steep, rough incline. The horses could not pull the wagon up without stopping to rest every few feet. Mary was to block the wheels with boulders when they halted so the wagon would not roll back down. She spent the afternoon lugging the big rocks up the slope, blocking the wheels, and lugging them some more. The two youngest children needed help up, too, and Mary gladly carried them to the top. But when the wagon and the family reached level ground at last, she was trembling and sick from exhaustion. From that day on, her health was never the same. For the rest of the trip, she could not walk more than a few yards without weakness and trembling overcoming her, and she was almost always very tired.

Beyond Salt Lake, the Powerses met a "sheep train"—a small company driving a flock of sheep west. Traveling with them for a few days, Mary befriended them, although her husband remained distant and angry. Mr. Curtis, who owned part of the flock, couldn't help noticing Dr. Powers's peculiar behavior, and quietly assured Mary that he and the others would care for her and the children. This was the most dangerous part of the route, he told her, and she needn't fear being abandoned. He talked Dr. Powers into borrowing some of their horses, and shared their precious dried beef and cheese. Mary gratefully repaid their kindness with a bar of soap and used the last of her dried strawberries and nutmeg to make them a shortcake.

Soon the party met a wagon train going to California, where the Powerses were headed. Mr. Curtis helped Dr. Powers contract to travel with the company. Seeing the family's obvious distress, the company agreed to escort the Powers across the desert country ahead. A capable traveler named Major Whitesides abandoned his wagon and put his belongings into the Powerses' wagon so they could use his oxen. He drove, relieving a weak and tired Mary of the responsibility.

The wagon train crossed the vast, dangerous deserts of today's Nevada. Mary watched another horse die in agony, despite her feeding him precious flour, and she made coffee out of such foul-tasting water that she never liked coffee again. Ever thoughtful of her children, she tucked away a large bottle of clear water for them and rationed it out sparingly when all the other water was gone. At night, she lay awake in the wagon while the others slept. Worry and fear clouded her mind, and since the family had long ago stopped setting up their sleeping tent she was cramped between her husband and children. Always weary, she sometimes took afternoon naps in the hot, lurching wagon.

By the time they reached the Sierra Nevadas, the Powerses' contract with the wagon train had expired, and the family was traveling alone again. They had been offered a donkey that was hitched with their last remaining horse, Blackey. Struggling over the jagged mountains, Mary continued to care for her family, even though her health was poor. Once again, their flour was gone.

Finally, on October 8, 1856, they inched into the Sacramento Valley. Mary remembered feeling desperate to get out of the wagon, but when she tried to walk, she trembled so badly she could hardly stand. Using a stick for a cane, she struggled down the last hill, hearing her husband's shouts to hurry up, but not being able to respond. When she reached the others, she was so weak she had to be lifted into the wagon where she lay until she had to get supper.

California was rich with harvest foods, and the half-starved family delighted in the tomatoes, cabbage, beets, and watermelon that other settlers shared with them. As Mary tried to regain her strength, she thanked God for sparing her three treasured children on the long, hard journey.

The Powerses took a boat down the river to a tiny cabin near San Leandro, California. This would be their home, and Mary said that despite its miserable floor, the cabin had a good roof and she made it "quite comfortable." Dr. Powers planted potatoes, which thrived in the dark soil. Mary wrote about how hard he worked to provide for his family and how devoted he had become since they settled down.

Mary rejoiced when she found letters from home at the post office. She was thrilled to receive a trunk that had been sent by ship, filled with desperately needed clothing and other supplies. Everywhere she went, she made new friends. She tried to improve her health, but the grueling overland trip had taken a terrible toll on her, and day-to-day frontier life was demanding. As she struggled to cope, she realized she was pregnant.

The following June, twins were born to the Powerses. The babies were beautiful and alert, and Mary adored them. Despite her fatigue, she rocked and held them day and night. But within six months, both infants had died, probably of illness, although Mary's writings do not tell us. She grieved with all her heart.

Mary seemed to know her own life was near its end. She wrote home: ". . . but dear mother I much fear we shall never meet again except in the spirit land . . ." Two months later, on May 1, 1858, Mary died.

Even on the verge of death, Mary continued to care for her three older children. Her last wish was that they be sent East to be brought up and educated by her mother. Perhaps it is best that Mary never knew that two of them would die in childhood and the third, Sarah, would grow up in the wilds of California with little opportunity for education or culture. Sarah taught herself to write by copying her grandmother's letters.

Mary Rockwood Powers endured—with courage and restraint—a chilling journey that today we can hardly imagine. Despite the anguish of the trip, she devoted herself to her loved ones and learned to take charge when her husband's unstable behavior endangered the family's welfare. Through her letters and diary we have a clear picture of this remarkable woman who sacrificed her health bringing her family safely across the overland trail. ▦

Specific Sources for Mary Rockwood Powers's Story

Malone, Michael P., editor. *Historians and the American West*. Lincoln and London: University of Nebraska Press, 1983.

Powers, Mary Rockwood. *A Woman's Overland Journey to California*. Fairfield, Washington: Ye Galleon Press, 1985.

Powers, W. P., compiler. *Some Annals of the Powers Family*. Los Angeles, California, 1924.

A HONEYMOON
TRIP TO MONTANA

The Story of Ellen Gordon Fletcher

Ellen Gordon Fletcher leaned back in her covered wagon's comfortable arm chair. Through the opening in the white canvas overhead, she could see a perfect rainbow glowing against the gray Wyoming sky. The enticing smells of frying bacon and wood smoke drifted into the cozy wagon. Billy was cooking breakfast again. For a few moments, she snuggled inside her woolen shawl, warm and contented.

To twenty-five-year-old Ellen (known to her family as "Nellie"), this 1866 honeymoon trip to Montana Territory's famous gold camp, Virginia City, was the experience of a lifetime. She was a New York schoolteacher who had met thirty-seven-year-old William Asbury Fletcher when he fell ill during a trip East from the Montana mining towns. He had started a butcher shop near Virginia City and wanted to return there. Ellen nursed him back to health, and the two were married in April, 1866.

Shortly after their wedding, they left New York by train, later taking a steamer up the Missouri River to Bellevue, Nebraska. From there they would have to continue the journey to Montana Territory by covered wagon. Packed and ready, they lumbered their slow way along the north bank of the Platte River on the Old Mormon Trail. Beyond Fort Laramie, in the southeast corner of today's state of Wyoming, they turned off onto the new and dangerous Bozeman Trail.

The "bloody Bozeman" was indeed a hazardous route for settlers to take. The Sioux nation had recently conquered the surrounding territory from the Crow people, and considered it prime hunting grounds. But the United States Congress wanted this comparatively short, easy route to the Montana gold fields open to settlers and suppliers. Bloodshed resulted.

Even when they saw evidence of warfare, though, Ellen felt safe. William Fletcher, whom she affectionately called Billy, was a strong, capable traveler who could afford the necessities of the long journey. He had prepared for the trip with well-built wagons, hardy mules, and hundreds of pounds of supplies—five hundred pounds of flour alone.

Certain that their healthy animals could handle the heavy load, the Fletchers had added a few luxuries to make the trip more pleasant. Before leaving Nebraska, they purchased three pretty fabric-bottomed folding chairs, including an arm chair for the wagon. Along with the ordinary food staples, they carried four dozen cans of peaches as well as oysters, blackberry wine, and syrup. There was vinegar and molasses, and dried fruit (apples, peaches, currants, and prunes) to go with their supplies of codfish, bacon, and ham. They even brought their opera glass for looking at distant objects.

Ellen watched the rainbow fade from the sky. She could hear the soft voices of Billy's sister, Chell (Rachel), and his daughter from an earlier marriage, Ella, outside. There were other sounds, too. A jay in the nearby scrubby undergrowth called to the campers. Horses nickered. Others in the train of twenty-five wagons were hitching up or preparing coffee over snapping fires. Once in a while, Ellen could hear her brother Will and Billy's brother Townie taking care of the mules.

As she pulled her long dress and warm shawl closer, perhaps Ellen wondered if she was already expecting a child. She and Billy had been married about two months, and she had been feeling rather tired lately. It was nice that he made the morning fire and breakfast, letting her sleep. Such kindness was typical of him. In fact, the whole Fletcher group had traveled in harmony, sharing the chores and doing small courtesies for each other since they left the banks of the Missouri in May.

Ellen straightened up the wagon. Before stepping out into the crisp, pungent morning air for breakfast and coffee with her husband, she sat down and penciled a few lines in her small leather-covered diary, beginning with her usual Scripture verse. Later in the day she would add to the long letter she was writing to her family back home.

The route they were traveling to Virginia City had a short but violent history of conflict, for despite the angry Sioux, who considered wagon travelers invaders into their pristine hunting territory, emigrants continued to use it. In addition to the plentiful grass and water for livestock, the Bozeman Trail was perhaps four hundred miles shorter than the alternate route.

The Fletchers' timing was exceptionally fortunate. At almost exactly the same time their party (which had joined a larger wagon train to increase their numbers) turned onto the Bozeman Trail, United States government agents were at Fort Laramie attempting to make a treaty with the Sioux. The treaty would officially open the trail to emigrants. Although many tribal leaders refused to attend the council, charging that the government intended to open the route with or without their consent, most were clustered near the fort. The Fletcher party slipped over the Bozeman Trail while the Sioux people were thus otherwise occupied. Earlier and later Bozeman Trail travelers encountered the tribe's fury over the invasion. Only two years later, led by famous Chief Red Cloud, the Sioux triumphed in closing the Bozeman Trail and the new military forts along the route.

Ellen wrote with fascination, but without fear, about the hundreds of Native Americans they did encounter on the trip. Their ways intrigued her, and she conversed comfortably with them, once trading a cup of sugar for a pair of beaded moccasins. She asked to see the long ornaments they wore in their ears, describing the bright-colored beads and shells fastened to the ends. Once she watched the women putting up tepees, writing home that the lodges were "made of elk skins nicely pieced together, and looked very novel and pretty to me, with the poles sticking out of the top."

Ellen's enthusiastic letters reflected her congenial, lighthearted spirit. She and Billy were happy, the traveling (although difficult) was exciting, and new sights greeted her daily. She wrote page after page, especially to her sisters whom she missed very much, painting word pictures, like her description of one night's camp:

> It was a pretty sight, the circular correll of white topped wag-
> ons and tents scattered here and there, the blazing fires shin-
> ing through the trees, the busy men and women hurrying to
> and fro, and the quiet moon looking down over it all. A large
> tree, bent over like an arch, crowns our wagon. I could'nt help
> wishing that you could overlook the scene. . . .

She wrote that her husband brought her pretty bouquets of wildflowers, told of enjoying hot, savory oyster soup and roast antelope on the road, and described the awe-inspiring scenery, inviting her family to join them out West. Often she enclosed flowers she pressed along the route, tiny chips of colorful agate, or later, sparkling flecks of Virginia City gold in her letters.

ELLEN GORDON FLETCHER
COURTESY OF GRANDEE PRINTING CENTER, INC.

While her letters usually bubbled with enthusiasm, Ellen sometimes elaborated on the less pleasant aspects of the journey in her diary. The weather was freezing cold at times or unbearably hot, and the bad road was enough to break sturdy wagon axles, causing delays. She told of mosquito swarms, irritating burrs that stuck to her clothing, and a dreadful toothache Billy endured. She mentioned in one shaken paragraph that her capable husband nearly drowned at a dangerous stream crossing but was rescued with ropes thrown to him. And she was distressed when, contrary to her beliefs as a devout Methodist, it was necessary to work or travel on the Sabbath.

The group pressed on, crossing the Powder, Tongue, Bighorn, and Yellowstone rivers in today's Wyoming and southern Montana. Ellen sometimes rode in the wagon, but other times she walked or rode horseback. She admired the green mountain valleys and the rushing streams, writing that this was "the finest country I have ever yet seen." Groups of Arapaho and Cheyenne clustered around the wagons wanting to trade. The trail was so steep in places that some emigrants actually switched the wheels on their wagons, putting the two large back wheels on the downhill side and the smaller front wheels on the uphill side to prevent roll-overs. Teams were doubled. Ellen reported walking over the final perpendicular, washed-out stretch of road that led, at last, to Virginia City. They arrived on July 27, 1866.

In her letters, Ellen described the far-flung little town, seeing the brown, stripped hills and the ugly diggings, but also mentioning the "very fine stone buildings, quite stylish and city-like" and the smallest houses she had ever seen—which reminded her of chicken coops— "built right on the mountain side."

After a few days, they continued several miles up into the mountains to another small gold camp where the butcher shop Billy had established earlier with his brother Townie was located. There they found a two-room cabin to live in while Billy began building a log house. He chose a spot on a steep mountainside where the view, according to Ellen, was "splendid." From her temporary cabin, she watched the miners work for gold with their sluice boxes. She was amused by their bachelor lifestyle. Most lived in tiny makeshift huts and ate bakery-purchased pies and meat on a stick. She said that some of the men were "real gentlemen" despite their reputation for drinking and carousing.

For entertainment, she sifted through the mine tailings to find small semi-precious garnets, and visited the other women of the settlement. When Billy finished their log house, they moved in. Ellen described their rustic handmade furniture and warm feather beds and pillows. Food prices were high, but from Ellen's letters it seems as though they had supplies left over from the trip, and money enough to buy what they needed.

Typically gold camps had short lives, and before long the initial mining boom in Virginia City and the surrounding camps began to fade. Billy and Townie decided to ranch in the warmer nearby Madison Valley. There they built another snug log house and a stable on the wide, golden rangeland surrounded by purple mountains. Ellen joined them, and eventually this beautiful valley with its sweeping vistas became their permanent home.

On March 5, 1867, Ellen and Billy's first child, Blanche, was born. It is almost certain that Ellen was, after all, expecting her baby on the wagon journey, but like most pioneer women, was reserved about discussing such private matters even in her diary.

Little Blanche delighted her parents, and during the following years was joined by several younger brothers and sisters. Ellen and Billy ranched, made and sold butter, taught Sunday School, continued the butchering business, and raised their large family in the cradle of the Madison Valley. One of Ellen's letters tells of riding "well wrapped up with blankets and buffalo robes" to a neighboring ranch to celebrate

Christmas. For many years, the warm, busy Fletcher home was a favorite stop for friends and customers alike. Today, the family is remembered for being true Montana pioneers.

Ellen Gordon Fletcher was a literate, adventurous young woman when she passed unharmed over the Bozeman Trail. She carefully recorded the details of her trip, which became lifelong memories and a treasured heritage to pass down to her children and grandchildren. A devoted mother and a sunny, descriptive writer, Ellen became a historian in her own way. With her detailed writings, she put down on paper forever her rare account of what it was like to be a bride on the Bozeman Trail. ▨

Specific Sources for Ellen Gordon Fletcher's Story

Haines, Jr., Francis D., editor. *A Bride on the Bozeman Trail/ The Letters and Diary of Ellen Gordon Fletcher/ 1866.* Medford, Oregon: Gandee Printing Center, Inc. 1970.

Johnson, Dorothy M. *The Bloody Bozeman/ The Perilous Trail to Montana's Gold.* New York, Toronto: McGraw-Hill Book Company, 1971.

Madison County History Association, compilers. *Pioneer Trails and Trials: Madison County 1863-1920.* Madison County History Association, 1976.

Montana Historical Society Archives, Small Collection 78: The Ellen Fletcher Papers.

Sievert, Ken and Ellen. *Virginia City and Alder Gulch.* Helena, Montana: Montana Magazine and American & World Geographic Publishing, 1993.

ADDITIONAL SOURCES

Brown, Dee. *The Gentle Tamers/Women of the Old Wild West*. Lincoln and London: University of Nebraska Press, 1981. (Originally published New York: Putnam, 1958.)

Editors of Time-Life Books with text by Joan Swallow Reiter. The Old West Books. *The Women*. New York: Time-Life Books, 1979.

Editors of Time-Life Books with text by Huston Horn. The Old West Books. *The Pioneers*. New York: Time-Life Books, 1976.

Faragher, John Mack. *Women and Men on the Overland Trail*. New Haven: Yale University Press, 1979.

Holmes, Kenneth L., editor and compiler. *Covered Wagon Women/Diaries and Letters from the Western Trails 1840-1890*, volumes I - XI. Glendale, California, 1983-1988, and Spokane, Washington, 1989-1993. The Arthur H. Clark Company.

Myres, Sandra L. *Westering Women and the Frontier Experience, 1800-1915*. Albuquerque, New Mexico: Univ. of New Mexico Press, 1982.

National Geographic Society, Special Publications Division. *Trails West*. Washington, D.C.: National Geographic Society, 1979.

Ross, Nancy Wilson. *Westward the Women*. New York: Alfred A. Knopf, 1944.

Schlissel, Lillian. *Women's Diaries of the Westward Journey*. New York: Schocken Books, Inc., 1982.

Museums:
End of the Oregon Trail Interpretive Center, 1726 Washington Street, Oregon City, Oregon.

Clark County Historical Museum, 1511 Main Street, Vancouver, Washington.

Old College Hall Museum, Pacific University, Forest Grove, Oregon.

Old Fort Hall Replica, Pocatello, Idaho.

Audio/visual:
In Search of the Oregon Trail. Producer/director Michael Farrell. PBS documentary. Co-produced by Oregon Public Broadcasting and the Nebraska ETV Network.

Maps:
The Oregon Trail: Transforming the West, fifth edition, 1995. Produced by the Oregon Trail Coordination Council. Karen Bassett, illustrator. Jim Johnston, American Adventures Press, producer.

Western Emigrant Trails 1830-1870: Major Trails, Cutoffs, and Alternates, second edition, 1991, 1993. Published by the Oregon-California Trails Association. Robert L. Berry, Map Project Editor. James A. Bier, Cartographer.

INDEX

ABOUT THE AUTHOR

Mary Barmeyer O'Brien was born and raised in Missoula, Montana, and received a B.A. from Linfield College in McMinnville, Oregon. She is also the author of *Jeannette Rankin: Bright Star in the Big Sky*, a biography for young readers. Her magazine articles for both children and adults have appeared in many national publications including *NorthwestLiving!*, *Ladies' Home Journal*, *Jack and Jill*, *Catholic Parent*, *Living with Preshcoolers*, and *Glacier Valley*. Mary works from her home in Polson, Montana, where she lives with her husband, Dan, who is a high school biology teacher, and their three children, Jennifer, Kevin, and Katie.